Silent Signals:
"Mastering the Art of Nonverbal Communication"

How to unlock the Hidden Power of Body Language, Facial Expressions, and Gestures

Gary Everson

Copyrights© Gary Everson

All rights reserved. No part of this book may be used or reproduced in any form whatsoever without written permission form the author or her publishers except in the case of brief quotations in critical articles or reviews.

TABLE OF CONTENTS

INTRODUCTION

CHAPTER ONE
The Language Beyond Words

CHAPTER TWO
Decoding Body Language

CHAPTER THREE
The Power of Facial Expressions

CHAPTER FOUR
Gestures that Speak Volumes

CHAPTER FIVE
The Art of Eye Contact

CHAPTER SIX
The Dynamics of Personal Space

CHAPTER SEVEN
Mastering the Art of Posture

CHAPTER EIGHT
Understanding the Role of Gestures

CHAPTER NINE
The Subtle Power of Tone and Voice

CHAPTER TEN
The Influence of Touch

CHAPTER ELEVEN
The Role of Proxemics in Communication

CHAPTER TWELVE

The Impact of Silence in Communication

CHAPTER THIRTEEN

Interpreting Cultural Differences in Nonverbal Communication

CHAPTER FOURTEEN

The Influence of Nonverbal Communication in Professional Settings

CHAPTER FIFTEEN

Enhancing Relationships Through Nonverbal Communication

CHAPTER SIXTEEN

The Future of Nonverbal Communication in a Digital Age

NOTES

THIS PAGE IS INTENTIONALLY LEFT BLANK

INTRODUCTION

In an age where spoken words often take center stage, the subtle art of nonverbal communication is frequently overlooked. However, these unspoken signals—comprising body language, facial expressions, and gestures—carry profound weight, shaping our interactions and influencing how we connect with those around us. **"Silent Signals: Mastering the Art of Nonverbal Communication"** seeks to illuminate this hidden dimension of human interaction, offering you a roadmap to harness its power effectively in both personal and professional settings.

The Unspoken Language

Nonverbal communication—the nuanced transmission of messages without the use of words—encompasses a diverse range of silent cues. This includes body language, facial expressions, and gestures, all of which often communicate more than spoken words. Mastering this silent language enables you to navigate complex social interactions with greater ease, helping you to discern true feelings and intentions that might otherwise remain hidden.

Why Nonverbal Communication Matters

Interactions are a blend of verbal and nonverbal elements. While spoken words convey explicit messages, it is the accompanying nonverbal cues that often provide deeper insight into our emotions and intentions. By developing proficiency in interpreting and employing these signals, you can enhance your ability to negotiate effectively, strengthen interpersonal relationships, and navigate various social contexts with greater confidence.

"**Silent Signals**" aims to deepen your understanding of nonverbal communication, emphasizing its crucial role in human interactions. Whether your goal is to improve personal relationships, advance professionally, or simply become more perceptive of social dynamics, mastering nonverbal communication can significantly enrich your interactions and outcomes.

What You Will Discover

This book offers a structured approach to exploring nonverbal communication, blending theoretical insights with practical applications. Here's what you can expect to learn:

Understanding Body Language: Delve into the multifaceted aspects of body language, from posture and movement to the concept of proxemics (spatial awareness). Discover how these nonverbal signals can reveal underlying attitudes and emotions.

Deciphering Facial Expressions: Gain insight into the subtleties of facial expressions and how they convey complex emotional states. Learn to recognize and interpret these cues to enhance your understanding of others' true feelings.

Mastering Gestures: Explore the role of gestures in communication. Understand how to use gestures effectively to support and enhance your verbal messages, and how to read the gestures of others to gain a fuller picture of their intentions.

Applying Your Knowledge: Acquire practical strategies for applying your understanding of nonverbal communication in various settings, including personal interactions, professional environments, and public speaking scenarios.

Building Awareness: Develop self-awareness of your own nonverbal signals and their impact on your interactions. Learn how to align your body language, facial expressions, and gestures with your verbal communication to present a consistent and authentic message.

The Journey Ahead

Mastering nonverbal communication is not just about decoding others' silent signals but also about using this knowledge to enhance your own communication skills. **"Silent Signals"** will guide you through this journey, showing you how to build rapport, navigate social complexities, and influence outcomes with subtlety and precision.

As you delve into the chapters of this book, you will uncover the transformative power of nonverbal communication, equipping yourself with the tools to connect more deeply, persuade effectively, and thrive in all your interactions. Welcome to a journey where silence speaks volumes, and where mastering the art of nonverbal communication opens doors to richer, more meaningful connections.

CHAPTER ONE

The Language Beyond Words

Beyond merely spoken or written words, communication also involves a complex web of nonverbal clues that have a significant impact on our interactions. The silent language of posture, gestures, facial emotions, and spatial orientation is known as nonverbal communication. It is a potent addition to spoken communications, frequently revealing more nuanced aspects of our feelings and intentions.

The capacity of nonverbal communication to support or contradict spoken statements is an important feature. For example, there is a contradiction between a person's words and their nonverbal cues when they claim to be cheerful yet exhibit tense body language, like a rigid posture or a forced smile. This mismatch can uncover underlying unease or lies, providing a more complex picture of their actual emotions.

Our ability to communicate and read others is greatly influenced by our body language. Our level of engagement and comfort is communicated through handshakes, nods, and even how we occupy our personal space. Whereas a feeble handshake could imply insecurity, a forceful one might convey confidence. Analogously, extending forward during a discussion usually denotes curiosity, while bending backward may show indifference or unease.

Nonverbal communication also includes important aspects of facial expressions. Numerous emotions, ranging from happiness and surprise to rage and grief, can be seen on our faces. The Duchenne smile—a sincere smile that meets the eyes—is frequently interpreted as an expression of sincere joy. A grin without involving the eyes, however, could be seen as polite but insincere.

Communication can also be affected by our use of eye contact. Eye contact can convey a variety of messages, such as respect and attentiveness, but it can also indicate discomfort or disinterest. That being said, these activities are heavily influenced by cultural conventions. Although it may be viewed as rude or aggressive in some cultures, making direct eye contact is valued as a sign of honesty in others.

The way humans use and perceive physical space during interactions is known as spatial orientation, or proxemics. Context and culture influence how comfortable we are with personal space. Maintaining a certain distance in professional contexts can be essential for comfort and respect, but in intimate circumstances, near proximity might be appropriate. Comprehending these spatial limits facilitates more effective relationship navigation and helps prevent miscommunication.

In general, nonverbal cues provide human relationships a deep, frequently unconscious level of significance. Our capacity to communicate clearly and empathically can be improved by being aware of these subtle cues, which help us comprehend the feelings and intentions of others.

CHAPTER TWO

Decoding Body Language

Body language, which includes posture, gestures, and spatial orientation, is a dynamic and complex kind of nonverbal communication. These nonverbal clues are typically more informative than spoken words alone, and they provide insightful information about an individual's goals, attitudes, and feelings.

An essential component of body language is posture. It conveys our emotional state and degree of participation in a discussion. An open, straight posture, for instance, usually exudes confidence and focus. Slouching or crossing one's arms, on the other hand, could be interpreted as defensiveness, unease, or indifference. It is possible to deduce someone's emotional state and reaction to an interaction by paying attention to these postural clues.

Additionally, nonverbal cues like pacing, fidgeting, or clothing adjustments might disclose hidden feelings. While pacing may suggest restlessness or the desire to process information, fidgeting, on the other hand, may indicate worry or impatience. Conversely, methodical, steady motions frequently convey concentration and serenity. It is easier to grasp someone's emotional condition and behave appropriately when one can identify these bodily behaviors.

Physical space is used and perceived in interactions as part of spatial orientation, also known as proxemics. Situational context and cultural norms influence people's preferences for personal space. While it is desirable to keep a larger distance in certain cultures, close proximity is normal and even expected in others. Collectivists, for example, might feel more at ease in intimate social situations, whereas individualistic types might prefer more privacy. It is easier to respect people's comfort zones and promote understanding of these spatial conventions.

Understanding context is essential for deciphering body language. In certain contexts, a gesture or posture that is appropriate may not be appropriate in others. For instance, keeping eye contact informally could be interpreted as pleasant, but making too much of it in a formal meeting could be interpreted as aggressive. Effective and courteous communication is ensured by adapting our comprehension of body language to various settings.

We can improve our capacity to connect with people and handle social situations more skillfully by learning to read body language. With this knowledge, we can better comprehend nonverbal clues, modify our communication tactics, and forge stronger bonds with others.

CHAPTER THREE

The Power of Facial Expressions

A person's facial expressions can reflect a vast spectrum of emotions and states, making them an effective nonverbal communication tool. The 43 muscles in the human face allow it to create thousands of different expressions, each of which provides important clues about the emotions and reactions of the wearer.

Sincere feelings that words may not be able to convey are frequently conveyed through facial expressions. A sincere smile, or Duchenne smile, for instance, shows genuine warmth and satisfaction by using both the mouth and the eyes. A grin without a look in the eyes, on the other hand, could come across as fake or courteous but lacking emotion. To truly grasp someone's emotional condition, one must be able to distinguish these minute variations. In addition to smiling, other facial expressions that reflect different emotions include frowns, arched eyebrows, and squinted eyes. For instance, a frown usually conveys sadness or discontent, yet wide eyes and arched eyebrows can also convey shock or surprise. It enables us to react to other people's feelings in a kind and acceptable manner when we understand these sentiments.

The looks on people's faces vary greatly depending on their culture. Cultures differ in the degree and ways in which they exhibit certain emotions, even though certain feelings are known to all. To preserve social harmony, people may hide their emotions in certain cultures while openly expressing emotions is encouraged in others. It is easier to read facial expressions correctly and prevent miscommunication when one is aware of these cultural quirks.

Another important tool for controlling conversations is facial expression. A few nonverbal cues that indicate you are paying attention and participating in the conversation are keeping eye contact and nodding. A blank face or avoided eye contact, on the other hand, could indicate discomfort or disinterest. Management of conversation flow and improved communication effectiveness are made possible by an understanding of these dynamics.

In general, nonverbal communication relies heavily on facial expressions to convey a person's intentions and feelings. Our ability to communicate with others and handle emotional dynamics in a variety of situations can be enhanced by becoming proficient at reading facial expressions.

CHAPTER FOUR

Gestures that Speak Volumes

A dynamic component of nonverbal communication, gestures encompass a variety of motions and acts. These nonverbal cues can amplify or change the meaning of spoken words by expressing attitudes, emotions, and messages.

One of the most popular ways to communicate nonverbally is through hand gestures. Simple handshakes, waves, and thumbs ups can lend extra significance to spoken communications. A wave can be used to say hello or good-bye, although a thumbs up typically denotes agreement or approval. But the meaning of gestures can range greatly among cultures. For example, the hand sign for "OK" is considered favorable in many cultures but may be considered disrespectful in others. Understanding these cultural differences aids in clear communication and the prevention of misunderstandings.

Other gestures, such tapping fingers or crossing arms, convey attitudes and emotional states. For instance, crossing one's arms could imply defensiveness or discomfort, but tapping one's fingers could convey frustration or impatience. Acknowledging these nonverbal cues offers insightful information about an individual's emotional condition and facilitates proper response.

When reading gestures, context is also very important. A gesture that is appropriate in one context could not be in another. Giving someone a pat on the back, for instance, could be interpreted as supportive in a social situation but as condescending in a formal one. Using gestures correctly and efficiently requires an understanding of the context. Apart from hand gestures, additional body movements like shrugs, nods, and posture adjustments also add to the overall message. A shrug, on the other hand, could convey doubt or apathy, but a nod can convey agreement or acceptance. Observing these motions improves our capacity to decipher and react to nonverbal cues.

In general, gestures are an effective nonverbal communication tool that may express a variety of ideas and feelings. Accurately recognizing and interpreting gestures can improve our ability to communicate and forge closer bonds with people.

CHAPTER FIVE

The Art of Eye Contact

Making eye contact is a basic nonverbal communication technique that is essential for building engagement, connection, and trust. The way we use our eyes in encounters can have a big impact on how people interpret and perceive what we're trying to say.

Sustaining suitable eye contact demonstrates self-assurance and focus. It shows that you are genuinely interested in the other person and totally involved in the conversation. Making constant eye contact, for instance, throughout a conversation demonstrates that you are paying attention and appreciating what the other person has to say. Conversely, averting eye contact could be taken as indifference, unease, or even lying.

Eye contact customs are heavily influenced by cultural standards. Making direct eye contact is regarded as a show of respect and sincerity in certain cultures, but not in others. It could be seen as impolite or hostile. For instance, keeping eye contact is crucial in many Western cultures to convey involvement and honesty. On the other hand, extended eye contact could be viewed as rude or hostile in some Asian cultures. Understanding these cultural distinctions makes it easier to navigate cross-cultural relationships.

Maintaining eye contact also helps control the direction of the conversation. It can encourage the other person to keep talking by demonstrating that you are paying attention. Furthermore, maintaining eye contact helps control the dynamics of a conversation, including whether to talk, When to halt, and express agreement or disagreement.

Different signals can also be conveyed by the length and intensity of eye contact. Prolonged eye contact can convey a feeling of intimacy or intensity, whereas brief, sporadic eye contact may convey curiosity or attention. You can modify your eye contact to fit the situation and your relationship with the other person by being aware of these variances.

In general, eye contact is a potent nonverbal communication technique that affects how we relate to and engage with other people. Making good eye contact can help us communicate more effectively and create deeper, more meaningful connections with others.

CHAPTER SIX

The Dynamics of Personal Space

The physical separation we keep between ourselves and other people when interacting is known as personal space, or proxemics. It is important for nonverbal communication since it affects our level of comfort and engagement in different social situations.

Cultural norms about personal space differ. Close proximity is customary and denotes warmth and familiarity in certain cultures, yet keeping a wider distance is desired in others to guarantee comfort and respect. For instance, being physically near to someone is expected and shows friendship in many Mediterranean cultures. In contrast, a bigger personal space is upheld to guarantee privacy and comfort in many Northern European and North American societies. Being aware of these cultural variations makes it easier to navigate social situations and prevent awkward situations.

Our impressions of personal space are also influenced by the interaction's setting. We may feel more at ease in close quarters, like with close friends or relatives. On the other hand, it's important to keep a polite distance in formal or professional contexts. In a meeting, for example, standing too near to a coworker could be interpreted as improper or intrusive. It is easier to promote constructive connections and prevent misunderstandings when we modify our usage of personal space according to the situation.

Individual differences might also affect one's desires for personal space. While some individuals might feel more at ease in close quarters, others could want greater separation. These preferences can be influenced by variables like personality, past experiences, and environmental context. Assessing the right amount of personal space and modifying our behavior accordingly is made easier by observing signs like body language and facial expressions.

All things considered, good nonverbal communication depends on knowing and honoring personal space. More relaxed and fruitful encounters with people can be created by paying attention to individual preferences, contextual considerations, and cultural conventions.

CHAPTER SEVEN

Mastering the Art of Posture

One of the most important aspects of nonverbal communication is posture, which conveys our attitudes, feelings, and degree of participation. Our body language during encounters might communicate confidence, openness, discomfort, or defensiveness, which can affect how other people interpret what we're trying to say.

Generally speaking, an open, erect stance conveys focus and assurance. An attitude of confidence and involvement can be projected by sitting or standing upright, shoulders back, and head held high. Adopting this posture not only improves our social status but also has a favorable impact on our self-esteem and mental state. For instance, when giving a presentation, standing up straight can help us come across to the audience as more personable and credible.

On the other hand, hunched over or closed posture can convey unease, defensiveness, or disinterest. Arm crossings, slouching, or leaning away from people can be signs of defensiveness or a lack of interest in the conversation. Accurately assessing others' emotional states and modifying our own posture are made easier when we are aware of these postural clues.

Additionally, posture controls how people interact with one another. During a conversation, for example, leaning forward typically indicates attention and attentiveness, but leaning back may indicate a more relaxed or disengaged position. Comprehending these postural dynamics enables us to effectively regulate the flow of conversations and react suitably to the cues of others. Posture affects group dynamics in addition to individual interactions. Posture in a group context can affect communication efficacy and cohesiveness. An open posture and eye contact with different group members, for instance, can encourage a feeling of inclusion and involvement, whereas a closed posture could obstruct efficient group communication.

In general, developing good posture strengthens our capacity for nonverbal communication and builds interpersonal connections. We may portray confidence, openness, and engagement by being aware of how our posture affects relationships, which promotes more fruitful and efficient communication.

CHAPTER EIGHT

Understanding the Role of Gestures

In nonverbal communication, gestures are an essential element that express a multitude of intents, feelings, and messages. The meaning of spoken words can be improved upon or changed by them, giving our relationships more depth and context.

Nonverbal communication is most commonly achieved through hand gestures, such as pointing, waving, or giving the thumbs up. Both spoken and nonverbal meanings can be communicated using these gestures. One way to express agreement or approval is with a thumbs-up, whilst greetings or goodbyes can be sent with a wave. Still, cultural differences can lead to disparate interpretations of gestures. For example, the hand sign for "OK" is appropriate in several cultures but inappropriate in others. Using gestures responsibly and preventing misunderstandings are made easier by being aware of these cultural differences.

Nonverbal communication also involves gestures other than hand gestures, like body language or facial expressions. For instance, shrugging may convey doubt or apathy, but nodding can convey agreement or acceptance. By identifying and deciphering these nonverbal cues, we can improve our comprehension of the intentions and feelings of others. Understanding gestures requires context. In some situations, a gesture may be suitable, but not in others. In an informal context, giving someone a pat on the back could be interpreted as encouraging, but in a professional setting, it could be considered as condescending or invasive. Respectful and efficient use of gestures is aided by context awareness.

In general, good nonverbal communication depends on the ability to recognize and comprehend gestures. Understanding the varied meanings of gestures and modifying them according to the situation can help us improve our relationships and forge closer bonds with people.

CHAPTER NINE

The Subtle Power of Tone and Voice

The way we speak affects how our spoken words are understood, and tone of voice is one important aspect of nonverbal communication. It expresses attitudes, feelings, and intentions; it frequently changes or enhances the meaning of what we say.

Pitch, loudness, and speed are only a few of the vocal characteristics that make up voice tone. Every one of these components has a part in the overall impact and message. In contrast, a harsh or monotone voice may cause stress or lead to misunderstandings. For instance, a warm and welcoming tone can promote effective communication and create a positive atmosphere.

Pitch, or voice pitch, can be used to highlight important details and express various emotions. Whereas a lower pitch can suggest authority or seriousness, a higher pitch can convey enthusiasm or anxiety. Our capacity to engage listeners and convey information more dynamically is improved when we are proficient in pitch modulation. Messages are also sent through volume. It's possible to come across as forceful or controlling when you speak too loudly, and unclear or timid when you speak too softly. Assuring that our communications are heard and comprehended without causing discomfort or misunderstanding requires finding the ideal balance in volume.

Communication is impacted by speech rate as well. We risk coming across as hurried or nervous when we speak too fast, and patronizing or deliberate when we speak too slowly. To preserve clarity and engagement, speech speed should be modified according to the audience and circumstance.
When it comes to nonverbal communication, tone and voice are effective instruments that influence how our messages are understood.

We may improve our ability to communicate and build more powerful and productive relationships by being proficient with these voice components.

CHAPTER TEN

The Influence of Touch

A rich and complex component of nonverbal communication, touch can express a variety of feelings and ideas. It is important for how we communicate, show empathy, and build connection with people.

Touches of different kinds, like a pat on the back, hug, or handshake, have different functions in communication. One frequent way to greet someone or express agreement is with a handshake, which conveys professionalism and respect. Conversely, depending on the situation and the relationship between the parties, a hug might express warmth, comfort, or affection. Comprehending the diverse forms of touch facilitates its suitable and successful utilization in a range of social contexts.

The way that contact is interpreted and accepted is greatly influenced by personal preferences and cultural conventions. Touch can be used for certain purposes or connections in certain cultures, but it is also frequently and happily accepted in others. Touch, for example, is frequently seen as a symbol of warmth and closeness in Mediterranean cultures, whereas more restrained societies, such those in Northern Europe or East Asia, can engage in less physical contact. Touch-related interactions can be handled more sensitively and respectfully when people are aware of these cultural variations.

When deciding whether or not to touch someone, context is also very important. Touch might vary and be less frequent in more casual or intimate contexts, but it can also be minimal or restricted to handshakes in formal or professional ones. In a casual atmosphere, giving someone a pat on the back, for instance, can be considered improper at a business meeting but acceptable in a social one. It is ensured that touch is utilized responsibly and politely when one understands the situation.

In general, touch is an effective and expressive nonverbal communication method that can represent a variety of feelings and ideas. Through awareness of personal preferences, cultural norms, and contextual elements, we can utilize touch as a tool to improve our relationships and communication with others.

CHAPTER ELEVEN

The Role of Proxemics in Communication

Proxemics, or the study of personal space and spatial relationships, is a vital part of nonverbal communication that determines how we interact with others. It involves the physical distance we maintain throughout conversations and how this distance effects communication dynamics.

Individuals and civilizations differ greatly in their desires for personal space. Close proximity is customary and denotes warmth and familiarity in certain cultures, yet keeping a wider distance is favored in others to protect privacy and comfort. Closer physical proximity, for instance, is customary and indicates a feeling of confidence and connection in many Middle Eastern and Latin American cultures. By contrast, keeping a greater personal space is prized in many Western societies as a way to respect people's privacy and boundaries.

Gaining an understanding of these cultural differences facilitates more skillful navigation of social interactions and helps one avoid uncomfortable situations.

Another important component of proxemics is context. Personal space preferences can be influenced by the type of interaction, interpersonal relationships, and environment. Close friends or family are examples of intimate environments where people could feel more at ease in close quarters. To promote comfort and professionalism in formal or professional contexts, one must maintain a respectful distance. Positive interactions and the avoidance of misunderstandings are promoted when we modify our usage of personal space according to the situation.

Individual characteristics such as personality, environmental context, and past experiences can also impact one's preferences for personal space.

Understanding and respecting proxemics is crucial for effective nonverbal communication. By being aware of cultural norms, contextual factors, and individual preferences, we can improve our interactions and forge stronger bonds with others. Some people may prefer more personal space because of past experiences or cultural background, while others may feel more comfortable with closer interactions.

CHAPTER TWELVE

The Impact of Silence in Communication

Silence is a significant and sometimes undervalued part of nonverbal communication that transmits meaning and impact in numerous circumstances. It functions as a means of communication that can emphasize points, indicate pauses, or convey feelings.

Silence can be used for a variety of objectives in discussions. It can be used to indicate introspection or contemplation, enabling people to gather data and come up with answers. One way to show consideration and thoughtfulness is to wait a moment before answering a question. Long periods of silence, on the other hand, could imply unease, disapproval, or lack of interest. It is easier to understand and respond appropriately when one is aware of the context and length of a silence, By causing pauses that can strengthen the effect of spoken words, silence also contributes to nonverbal communication. One way to highlight important points and give the audience time to process the material is by strategically pausing a speech or presentation. This kind of quiet use can improve engagement and communication in general.

Silence perception is greatly influenced by personal preferences and cultural standards. While silence may be viewed as awkward or uncomfortable in certain cultures, it may also be cherished as a sign of respect or introspection in others. In many Asian cultures, for instance, remaining silent throughout a conversation is frequently regarded as a show of respect and consideration. Conversely, in Western societies, quietness could be perceived as a lack of interest or reaction. It is easier to navigate relationships and prevent misunderstandings when one is aware of these cultural variances.

When it comes to communicating a variety of messages and emotions, silence is a powerful nonverbal communication tool. And We can improve our ability to communicate and also handle encounters more skillfully if we comprehend its varied applications and interpretations.

CHAPTER THIRTEEN

Interpreting Cultural Differences in Nonverbal Communication

To avoid misunderstandings and ensure successful cross-cultural encounters, it is imperative to comprehend these distinctions. Nonverbal cues including gestures, facial expressions, and personal space are governed by distinct cultural conventions. Direct eye contact, for example, is welcomed in certain cultures but may be viewed as confrontational or disrespectful in others. Similar to this, depending on the culture, gestures like handshakes, nods, and other physical displays might indicate different things. For instance, while many Western cultures view the "OK" hand sign favorably, other Middle Eastern or South American cultures may find it disrespectful.

Cultural differences can extend to preferences for personal space. Close physical contact is customary in some cultures and denotes warmth and connection, while keeping a wider distance is desired in others to protect privacy and comfort. For instance, preserving a reasonable amount of personal space is prized in many European cultures, whereas tighter proximity is more typical in many African or Latin American cultures. Respecting others' boundaries and fostering relaxed relationships are made easier by having an understanding of these cultural standards.

Different civilizations also have different gestures and facial expressions. Although certain emotions, like happiness or sadness, are understood by all, there are differences in how these feelings are expressed and understood. For instance, while it may be acceptable in some cultures to express emotions honestly, it may be more common for people to hide their emotions in order to preserve social harmony.

Being mindful of cultural variations in nonverbal communication is crucial for interpreting body language accurately and avoiding misunderstandings. Awareness of these differences enhances our ability to communicate effectively across cultures, foster stronger relationships, and adapt to diverse social settings with greater ease.

CHAPTER FOURTEEN

The Influence of Nonverbal Communication in Professional Settings

Nonverbal communication is essential in professional contexts, impacting how we communicate with coworkers, clients, and superiors. It can improve or degrade our effectiveness, shape our professional image, and influence the dynamics of working interactions.

Body language and posture play a big role in how we are viewed in professional contexts. Maintaining an erect, open posture, for example, indicates confidence and alertness, whereas slouching or crossing the arms may indicate defensiveness or apathy. Similarly, appropriate eye contact and facial expressions improve engagement and communication, whereas a lack of eye contact or expression can be interpreted as disengagement or discomfort.

Gestures also have an impact on professional communication. Handshakes, for example, are a common way to greet or agree in business settings.

A firm handshake conveys confidence and professionalism, whereas a weak handshake may be viewed as a lack of assertiveness. Understanding and applying suitable gestures aids in the formation of positive impressions and the development of effective interactions.

Professional communication also requires careful consideration of tone of voice and vocal attributes. A pleasant and expressive tone can foster a positive atmosphere and reflect professionalism, whereas a harsh or monotone voice may cause misunderstandings or tension. Mastering vocal aspects including pitch, volume, and speed improves communication efficacy and aids in managing professional relationships.

Personal space and proximity are also important in working contexts. Maintaining proper personal space contributes to a polite and comfortable atmosphere.

Respecting others' personal space, for example, ensures that interactions are professional and non-intrusive in meetings or during interviews. Understanding and responding to personal space preferences depending on context and cultural norms helps to promote pleasant workplace dynamics.

Overall, nonverbal communication has a substantial impact on professional encounters and relationships. By being aware of our body language, gestures, tone of voice, and personal space, we may improve our professional performance, make a better impression, and negotiate workplace dynamics successfully.

CHAPTER FIFTEEN

Enhancing Relationships Through Nonverbal Communication

Nonverbal communication improves human relationships by transmitting emotions, establishing trust, and promoting connection. Understanding and efficiently employing nonverbal clues can help us strengthen relationships and engage with others.

Facial expressions are essential for communicating emotions and establishing connections. A genuine smile, for example, might convey warmth and approachability, resulting in pleasant interactions. Similarly, maintaining eye contact demonstrates attentiveness and respect, which contributes to the development of trust and rapport. Recognizing and responding to these nonverbal signs helps us connect with others on a deeper level.

Gestures and body language are also important factors in connection building. Simple gestures, such as a reassuring touch or open body language, can communicate support and understanding. For example, putting a hand on someone's shoulder during a difficult conversation might bring comfort and support. Understanding and adjusting to these gestures promotes helpful and meaningful partnerships.

Tone of voice and vocal attributes are critical in sustaining strong relationships. A friendly and supportive tone can establish ties and convey sincerity, but a harsh or dismissive tone may cause tension or misunderstandings. Being aware of our vocal tone and modifying it based on the situation and relationship promotes positive interactions and healthy connections, intimate space and proxemics are very important in intimate relationships. Respecting others' personal space and preferences promotes comfortable and courteous relationships. For example, being aware of how close we stand during conversations and altering our distance based on the relationship and circumstance promotes pleasant connections while avoiding discomfort.

Overall, nonverbal communication has a considerable impact on the quality and depth of human relationships. We may improve our interactions by being aware of and efficiently using facial expressions, gestures, tone of voice, and personal space.

CHAPTER SIXTEEN

The Future of Nonverbal Communication in a Digital Age

The digital age has changed the way we communicate, especially the importance and significance of nonverbal communication. As technology advances, understanding how nonverbal cues are affected and how to adapt is critical for maintaining productive interactions.

Digital communication platforms such as video calls, social media, and messaging applications have changed the nature of nonverbal communication. Video calls, for example, can transmit facial expressions, gestures, and tone of voice, but they may limit other components of nonverbal communication, such as spatial orientation and touch. Adapting to these restrictions and discovering efficient ways to express nonverbal clues in digital encounters is critical for sustaining clear and meaningful communication.

Social media and messaging apps introduce unique challenges and possibilities for nonverbal communication. Emojis, gifs, and other digital symbols often replace facial expressions and gestures in text-based exchanges, enabling users to express emotions and intentions. However, these digital representations can be ambiguous and may not always accurately reflect the sender's true feelings. Recognizing the limitations and nuances of digital nonverbal communication can enhance your ability to interpret messages correctly and reduce misunderstandings.

Additionally, technologies like virtual reality (VR) and augmented reality (AR) offer novel avenues for nonverbal communication. These immersive platforms have the potential to enhance digital interactions by providing more lifelike expressions, gestures, and spatial awareness, contributing to more effective and engaging virtual communication. Exploring and adapting to VR and AR technology can help create more interesting and successful digital interactions.

Overall, the future of nonverbal communication in the digital age depends on adjusting to new technology and understanding how they affect human interactions. We may improve our communication abilities and traverse the ever-changing environment of digital interactions by investigating and incorporating digital nonverbal clues and upcoming technology.

NOTES